Thank you so much for choosing our activity !
We truly hope that our book brings joy and

We would be honored if you could spare a moment to leave a review of our book. Your feedback is invaluable to us and helps us improve and reach more families in need of educational and entertaining resources.

Thank you again for choosing our activity book, and we can't wait to hear what you and your kids think!

This Book Belongs To

_ _

_ _

Welcome

To the

ACTIVITY BOOK FOR KIDS AGES 8-12 YEARS OLD

Prepare to embark on an incredible journey through the captivating pages of this Activity Book .

We've crafted this book with one goal in mind: to ignite your curiosity, challenge your intellect, and fill your days with endless fun!

Inside, you'll find an array of exciting activities, brain-teasing puzzles, and delightful games that will not only entertain but also educate. From navigating intricate mazes to solving challenging crosswords, from getting creative with coloring pages to tackling mind-bending math challenges and word searches, there's something here for every inquisitive mind.

So, without further ado,

let the adventure begin!

Landforms Word Search

Uncovering the hidden terms in the grid by looking in all directions, including backwards and diagonally

```
P B K P N G R B R W P M
V E W V P A Y S I A M T
Y V R C L R V G S T R P
S P G L A C I E R E I F
I E T V T N Z T S R V S
B N U O E I Y E L F E L
U I S L A N D O S A R F
E N R C U L O I N L Q N
B S L A K E L X Q L I T
K U S N T H N B J L G S
W L M O U N T A I N K D
V A L L E Y U G P H X R
```

Words to Finds

Mountain	Desert	Glacier
Valley	Volcano	Canyon
River	Peninsula	Plateau
Lake	Island	Waterfall

3

Space Crossword

Across grid answers shown: 5. ASTRONOMY, 8 (down) MOON

Across

4. The force that keeps planets in orbit around the Sun.

5. The study of stars, planets, and space.

6. A small, rocky planet closest to the Sun, named after the Roman messenger god.

8. The fourth planet from the Sun, often called the 'Red Planet'

9. The closest star to Earth.

Down

1. A giant ball of gas that shines brightly in the night sky.

2. The largest planet in our solar system, with a big red spot.

3. The _____ Galaxy is the large spiral of stars that includes our solar system.

7. The third planet from the Sun is called _____.

8. The shiny object that orbits Earth and reflects sunlight at night.

Maze #1

Can you guide the friendly Raccoon through the maze to reunite with his monkey buddy!

Sudoku #1

Easy

5			7				2	
		8	6					3
			5			1		6
			3			4	9	
1								5
	2	4			5			
2		6			3			
9					8	5		
	5				6			4

Easy

					7	1	3	
		6						
			9				2	
9	8			1				7
	3	4		8		5	6	
6				3			9	2
	4				3			
						2		
	7	9	4					

Medium

4					5		8	
9				8	7			6
			7		2			
		9				4	6	8
8	1	4			9			
		3		9				
2		1	7					3
	8		2					7

Medium

					5			
		1		8			7	5
	5			7		4		3
		9						4
	7		3		9		1	
1					6			
5		6	7					2
2	4		9			5		
			8					

Spot The Differences #1

Can you spot the 9 things that are different in these pictures?

Acrostic Poem #1

An acrostic poem is a type of poem where the first letter of each line spells out a word or phrase. All lines should relate to or Describe the poem.

Write an acrostic poem for the word below

GAME

G _____

A _____

M _____

E _____

Drawing Activity

Put your artistic talents to use by replicating the image with your own drawing skills

Anagram Challenge #1

Put your brain to the test and unscramble the names
of these countries!

Dniteu Mgidnko

- - - - - - - - - - - - - - - - - - -

Mnayger

- - - - - - - - - - - - - - - - - - -

Ulaiarsat

- - - - - - - - - - - - - - - - - - -

Htsou Rfcaai

- - - - - - - - - - - - - - - - - - -

Atrangine

- - - - - - - - - - - - - - - - - - -

Iodnasnei

- - - - - - - - - - - - - - - - - - -

Egg Mystery

What has hatched from the egg?

Math Challenge #1

Put your math skills to the test by solving these two-digit addition problems, using regrouping if needed

23
+ 35

47
+ 15

26
+ 30

18
+ 18

59
+ 20

88
+ 11

37
+ 22

55
+ 44

17
+ 65

75
+ 15

12
+ 16

31
+ 32

Guess the Country

Put your geography knowledge skills to the test!
Can you identify the african country from the clues given?

1. This country is located on the western coast of Africa.

2. It gained independence from France in 1960.

3. The official language spoken here is French.

4. Famous for its delicious cocoa beans and being one of the world's largest producers of cocoa

5. The the economic capital of this country is Abidjan.

Name

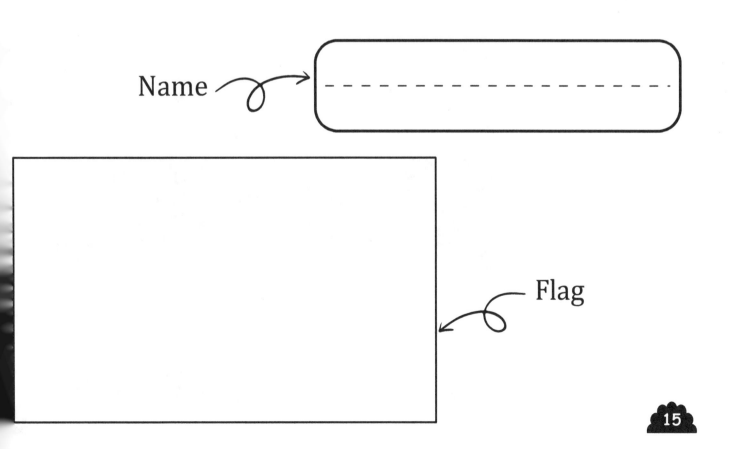

Flag

Assemble the Picture!

Can you piece together the picture? Find the right strips and assemble the image to complete the puzzle Write the numbers

Maze #2

The astronaut is lost in space and needs your help to find his way back to his ship. Use your skills to navigate through the vast galaxy and safely reunite him with his spacecraft

Mythical Creatures

Across

2. Giant with one eye from Norse mythology.

4. Half-human, half-horse creature.

6. Bird of fire that rises from its ashes.

8. Beautiful woman with the tail of a fish.

9. Mysterious, mischievous creature that grants wishes.

Down

1. Legendary creature that can turn to stone those who look into its eyes.

3. Small, mischievous fairy often depicted as a tiny person with wings.

4. Humanoid creature with wings and a bow and arrow, often associated with love.

5. Magical horse with a horn.

7. Fire-breathing serpent.

Ocean Life Word Search

Uncovering the hidden terms in the grid by looking in all directions, including backwards and diagonally

```
L  Q  A  S  T  A  R  F  I  S  H  K
D  M  L  E  E  G  A  S  I  R  N  B
I  A  U  S  E  A  W  E  E  D  I  P
P  F  Z  W  O  A  S  T  V  J  S  U
O  C  T  O  P  U  S  H  M  E  E  F
L  C  U  M  D  B  H  Q  E  L  V  F
P  J  R  K  O  X  A  O  X  L  H  E
K  C  T  L  L  Y  R  X  F  Y  L  R
U  C  L  W  P  G  K  G  Z  F  R  F
L  S  E  A  H  O  R  S  E  I  Y  I
N  O  B  Z  I  O  K  Z  H  S  T  S
C  L  O  W  N  F  I  S  H  H  D  H
```

Words to Finds

Dolphin	Seahorse	Lobster
Seashell	Octopus	Clownfish
Seaweed	Turtle	Pufferfish
Jellyfish	Starfish	Shark

Magnify The Ants

Sudoku #2

Easy

						2	6	
			4	5		8		
9				2				3
	9	7			6			
			3		7			
			1			6	4	
4				6				5
		2		1	8			
	1	9						

Easy

		1		8	6			
	7		5					
	9	5		4				
3			4					8
	2	4					9	1
	1				8			2
			5			6	2	
					3		9	
			2	6			5	

Medium

				9		4		
5				6	1	8		
			4			5	2	
6					2	7		
		7		3				
	4	3						1
4	7		5					
	1	5	9					4
		2		6				

Medium

	6	3			5	1		2
	5				6			4
1				9				
				2		3		
			7		1			
		6		5				
				1				8
3			9				6	
2		9	5			7	4	

Joke Decoding #1

Can you solve the secret code and uncover the hidden joke

a	b	c	d	e	f	g	h	i	j	k	l	m
1	2	3	4	5	6	7	8	9	10	11	12	13

n	o	p	q	r	s	t	u	v	w	x	y	z
14	15	16	17	18	19	20	21	22	23	24	25	26

Where do hamsters go on vacation?

H	a	m	s	t	e	r	d	a	m
8	1	13	19	20	5	18	4	1	13

What did the pig say on the beach?

I	a	m		b	a	c	o	n
9	1	13		2	1	3	15	14

What travels around the world but stays in one place?

a	S	T	a	M	P
1	19	20	1	13	16

What happens when you wear a watch on a plane?

T	I	M	E		F	L	I	E	S
20	9	13	5		6	12	9	5	19

Spot The Differences #2

Can you spot the 10 things that are different in these pictures?

Math Challenge #2

Put your math skills to the test and find the value of each emoji?

🐵 + ❤️ = 😦 + 1

😆 + 😆 = 🐵

5 = 😆 + 😦

😦 - 3 = 1

🐵 = [ ]   ❤️ = [ ]   😦 = [ ]

😆 = 3

Anagram Challenge #2

Put your brain to the test and unscramble these astronomy terms!!

ylagxa

_ _

lkacb eohl

_ _

ielcnlanottso

_ _

octepelse

_ _

arlso eystsm

_ _

suvienre

_ _

Wonders of a Giant Nose

What's coming out of this giant Nose?

Connect The Dots #1

Join the dots to unveil the picture

Dental Health

Across

3. Hidden part of a tooth beneath your gums.

5. Liquid used to rinse your mouth.

6. Device for cleaning your teeth.

10. Artificial set of teeth.

Down

1. Another name for a dental professional.

2. Tread to clean teeth

4. She might leave you money for your tooth

7. Tiny creature that can cause tooth decay.

8. An expert in clean teeth

9. Can give you cavities

Guess the Mythical Creature

Can you decipher the identity of the Mythical Creature based on the clues provided?

1. This mythical creature is known for its fiery nature and is often associated with flames and fire.

2. Legend has it that when this creature reaches the end of its life, it bursts into flames and is reduced to ashes, only to be reborn from those very ashes.

3. Its feathers are said to shine with brilliant colors, like red, orange, and gold.

4. In many cultures, it symbolizes immortality and the cycle of life, death, and rebirth.

5. This mythical bird is often depicted as a large and majestic creature, with a strong and noble appearance.

Name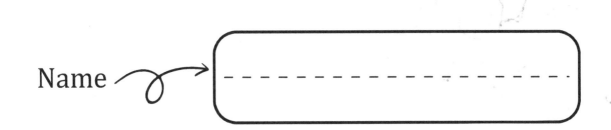

Maze #3

Will you help the bunny find his way?

Start

Finish

Story Starters

Max woke up one day to find that he could suddenly communicate with animals. The first animal to speak to him was his pet cat, Whiskers.

Drawing Activity

Put your artistic talents to use by replicating the image with your own drawing skills

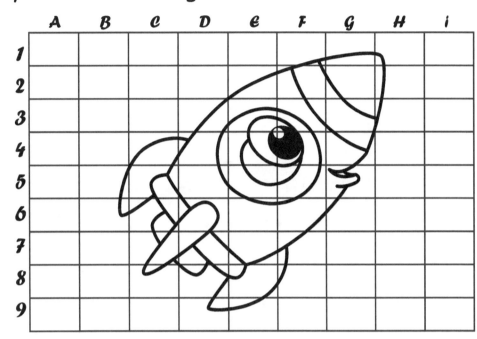

	A	B	C	D	E	F	G	H	i
1									
2									
3									
4									
5									
6									
7									
8									
9									

Can you spot the 10 things that are different in these pictures?

Halloween Word Search

Uncovering the hidden terms in the grid by looking in all directions, including backwards and diagonally

```
L A N T E R N G R A V E
I J F W M G P G R I N Z
M S K B T O I H N O H B
U Z P R D J N O T X S I
S C U O R C O S T U M E
T C M O F M B T T O J G
F O P M L M R Y F E Z G
O B K S O O O L I M R M
C W I T C H H B W L I B
X E N I V A M P I R E Z
D B K C R O W E E Y Y C
M X I K Z D N W V J V U
```

Words to Finds

Pumpkin	Ghost	Costume
Tombstone	Lantern	Zombie
Broomstick	Grave	Monster
Witch	Vampire	Cobweb

Boggle #1

How many words can you make using the letters below?

L	M	A	P
K	B	C	E
I	N	Y	S
F	G	V	O

_____   _____

_____   _____

_____   _____

_____   _____

_____   _____

_____   _____

_____   _____

_____   _____

_____   _____

Asian Culture Trivia Challenge

How much do you know about Asia? Answer the trivia questions and find out!

1. Which country is known for its traditional martial art form called Kung Fu?

    ○ China   ○ Japan   ○ India

2. Which Asian country is famous for its vibrant Bollywood film industry?

    ○ India   ○ South Korea ○ Thailand

3. Which Asian country is known for its intricate art of origami, the folding of paper into various shapes?

    ○ Japan   ○ China   ○ Thailand

4. Which country is home to the world's largest religious monument, Angkor Wat?

    ○ Cambodia ○ Vietnam   ○ Myanmar

5. Which Asian country celebrates the Lantern Festival, where people release colorful lanterns into the sky?

    ○ Taiwan   ○ Thailand ○ Malaysia

6. Which country in Asia is famous for its traditional tea ceremony?

    ○ Japan   ○ China   ○ South Korea

7. Which Asian country is known for its traditional dance form called Bharatanatyam?

    ○ India   ○ Indonesia ○ Philippines

8. Which Asian country is known for its vibrant festivals, such as Diwali and Holi?

    ○ India   ○ Japan   ○ Malaysia

9. Which country is famous for its traditional art of calligraphy, known as Shodo?

    ○ Japan   ○ China   ○ South Korea

Sudoku #3

Easy

		6	7	5				
						1	3	
3		8		6				2
8				7		6		
	7				8			
	3		5					4
9			4			6		8
	2	5						
				9	2	5		

Easy

4		2			1	9		6
7				8				
		3		4				
2						1		
		1	8		7	4		
		8						5
			2		6			
		7						8
9		4	3			5		7

Medium

	5							1
			5	2		8		
	6	1			9			
				6	3			7
	2			9			4	
5		3	4					
			9			2	3	
	7			3	4			
8							9	

Medium

	3		4	9				
5	4		2			9		7
	1							
	7	6	8					
1								3
				1	7	2		
							7	
3		7			2		5	4
			6	3		8		

41

Math Challenge #3

Put your math skills to the test! Use the numbers on the suitcase to solve multiplication problems and fill in the circles to create the perfect equation

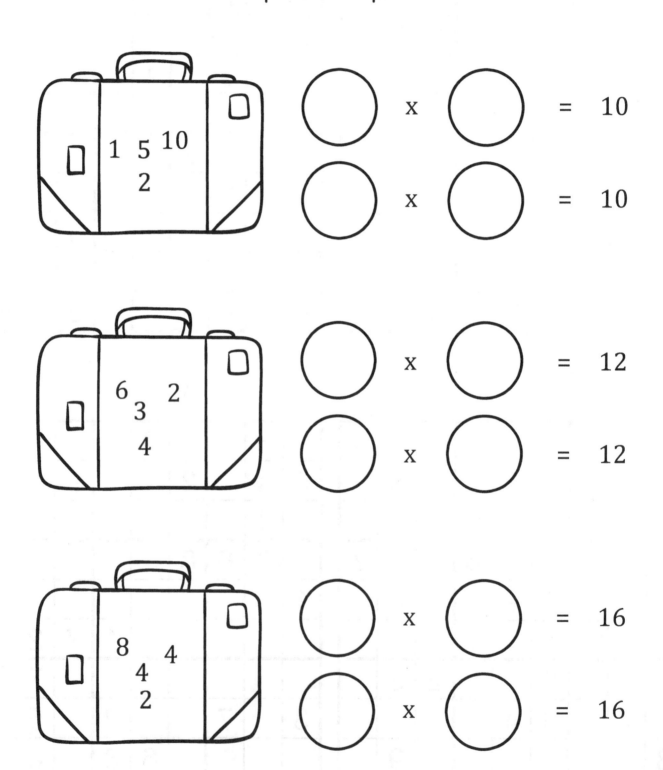

$\bigcirc$ x $\bigcirc$ = 10

$\bigcirc$ x $\bigcirc$ = 10

1 5 10
2

$\bigcirc$ x $\bigcirc$ = 12

$\bigcirc$ x $\bigcirc$ = 12

6   2
  3
   4

$\bigcirc$ x $\bigcirc$ = 16

$\bigcirc$ x $\bigcirc$ = 16

8   4
  4
  2

Connect The Dots #2

Join the dots to unveil the picture

Acrostic Poem #2

An acrostic poem is a type of poem where the first letter of each line spells out a word or phrase. All lines should relate to or Describe the poem.

Write an acrostic poem for the word below

Trees

T _____

R _____

E _____

E _____

S _____

What Is The Sloth Dreaming About?

Weather Crosswrods

Across

3. Drops of water that fall from the sky.

4. Flash of light during a storm.

6. Strong, swirling windstorm over land.

8. White flakes that fall in winter.

9. Cold, frozen rain.

Down

1. Thick fog that forms over bodies of water.

2. Swirling windstorm with a calm center.

5. Fluffy white water droplets in the sky.

7. Water droplets that form on cool surfaces at night.

8. Natural event with thunder, lightning, and heavy rain.

46

Guess the Landmark

Can you decipher the identity of the famous landmark based on the clues provided?

1. This iconic structure stands tall in the heart of a romantic city known for its croissants and art.

2. It was built for the 1887 World's Fair and was initially met with mixed opinions from the public.

3. Made of iron, it soars to a height of 330 metres (1,083 feet)), making it one of the tallest man-made structures of its time.

4. You can take an elevator ride to the top for breathtaking views or climb the stairs for a bit of exercise.

5. It twinkles with thousands of lights at night, creating a dazzling spectacle.

Name

Build A Giant Burger

Get ready to build your ultimate burger masterpiece! Using your favorite ingredients, toppings, and sauces, let your creativity soar and create a delicious burger that's unique to you

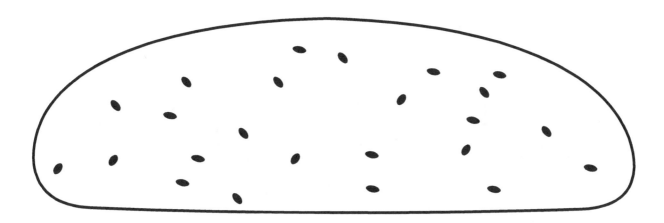

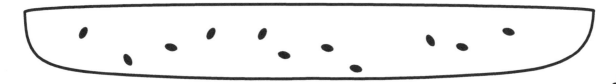

Maze #4

Can you assist the friendly bird in locating his most beloved tree

Drawing Activity

Mirror the image! Finish the right side of the picture by copying the lines from the left side

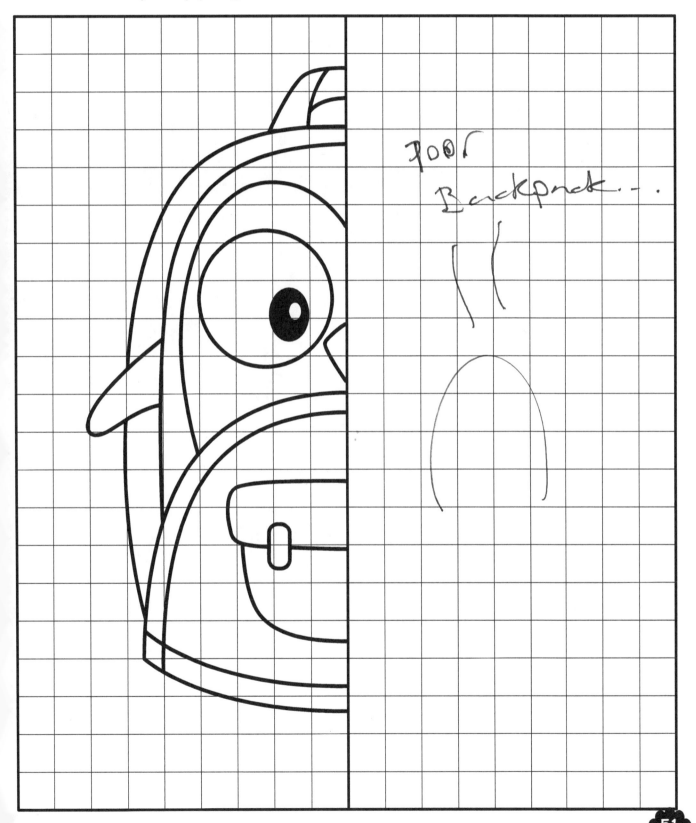

Can you spot the 10 things that are different in these pictures?

Anagram Challenge #3

Put your brain to the test and unscramble the name of these Vegetables!!

Clorboic

- - - - - - - - - - - - - - - - - - - -

Ubemucrc

- - - - - - - - - - - - - - - - - - - -

Trrcoa

- - - - - - - - - - - - - - - - - - - -

Ritnup

- - - - - - - - - - - - - - - - - - - -

Hnpsica

- - - - - - - - - - - - - - - - - - - -

Ioonns

- - - - - - - - - - - - - - - - - - - -

Mythical Creatures Word Search

Uncovering the hidden terms in the grid by looking in all directions, including backwards and diagonally

```
Z  Q  E  Q  G  H  Z  K  P  Z  Y  B
T  P  H  O  E  N  I  X  Q  N  N  O
I  M  I  N  O  T  A  U  R  L  D  U
B  W  E  G  R  I  F  F  I  N  Z  N
M  E  A  C  Y  C  L  O  P  S  P  I
K  R  A  K  E  N  C  A  E  C  O  C
D  E  F  R  R  N  X  Y  G  H  L  O
W  W  L  F  F  N  T  U  A  I  H  R
V  O  V  G  I  Z  J  A  S  M  F  N
F  L  N  H  S  P  Q  T  U  E  K  J
B  F  P  F  V  R  R  B  S  R  E  G
L  S  E  X  I  A  P  X  E  A  H  H
```

Words to Finds

Dragon	Minotaur	Pegasus
Unicorn	Cyclops	Sphinx
Phoenix	Kraken	Centaur
Griffin	Chimera	Werewolf

55

Robot Rampage

Draw an evil robot attacking the city

Join the dots to unveil the picture

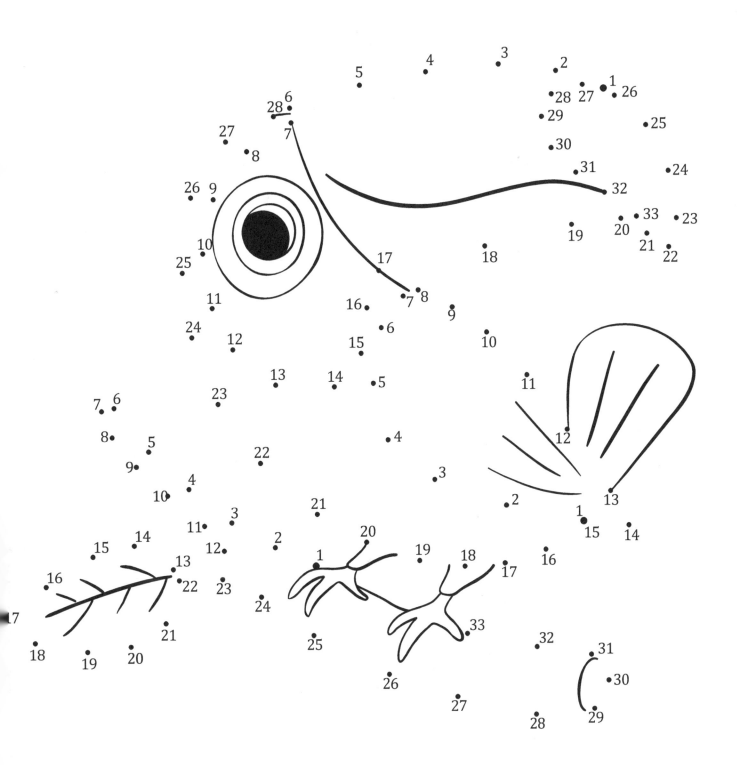

Math Challenge #4

Ball's in your court! Conquer these basketball-themed math challenges to become a Slam Dunk Math All-Star!

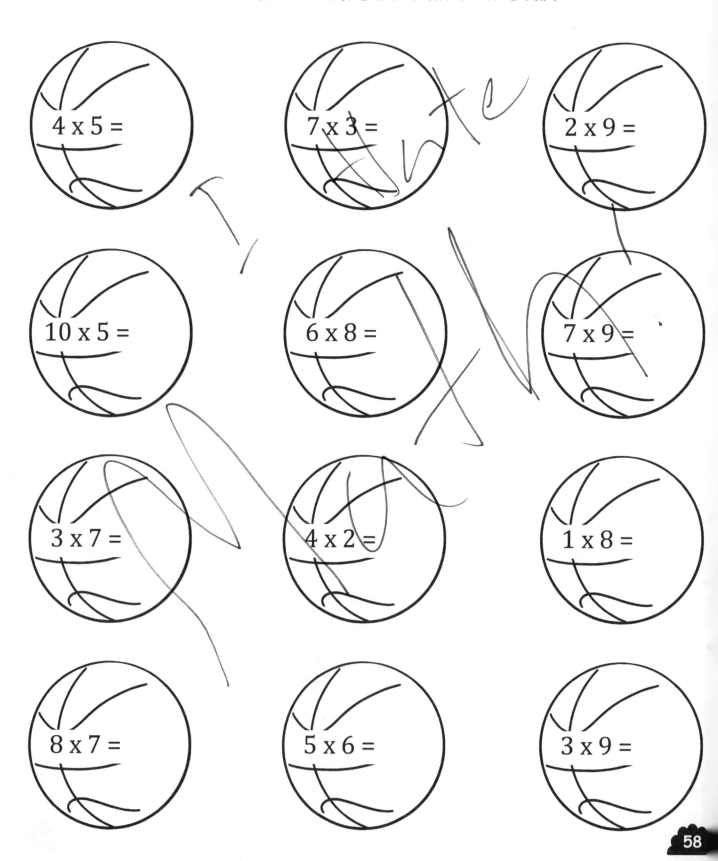

4 x 5 =

7 x 3 =

2 x 9 =

10 x 5 =

6 x 8 =

7 x 9 =

3 x 7 =

4 x 2 =

1 x 8 =

8 x 7 =

5 x 6 =

3 x 9 =

Make Your Own Monster

Sudoku #4

Easy

	3		1	9			2	
		4				6	5	
	9				8			
	8				9			
9		3				7		6
			2				9	
			8				7	
	5	9				4		
	4			2	6		1	

Easy

			4		3	7		
					7	5		
	9	5			6			
		7	9					
8	5						2	9
					5	6		
		5				4	1	
		3	7					
		1	8		2			

Medium

2	8	4					7	
		8						
			1	3	6	8		
			3			5	1	
			2					
	8	3			5			
4	2	5	6					
					1			
	6				7	9	4	

Medium

		1	4			3	9	
	7		5					
			1			2	6	
		7				1		
3		8		1		5		
	2					8		
1	4		9					
					7		1	
9	8				2	6		

Boggle #2

How many words can you make using the letters below?

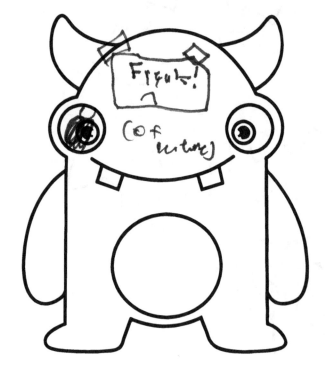

O	H	J	I
Z	W	X	A
E	D	R	Y
U	O	M	K

-------------------------------   -------------------------------

-------------------------------   -------------------------------

-------------------------------   -------------------------------

-------------------------------   -------------------------------

-------------------------------   -------------------------------

-------------------------------   -------------------------------

-------------------------------   -------------------------------

-------------------------------   -------------------------------

Family Members

Down

1. This is another word for a husband or wife

2. Children born to the same parents

4. The son of a brother or sister

5. This is a person related to us by blood

6. This is the son of your new husband or wife

7. A ..... aunt is a sister of our grandmother or grandfather

8. If somebody is your ..... brother or sister, they were born on the same day as you

Across

3. Family gatherings may include aunts, uncles, and ___

7. The parents of your parents

9. Someone who married into your family

In 20 Years...

By: Ashton katherin Powell

In 20 years, I will be dumber than 5 years old.

And my favorite hobby will be eating mayo straight from the jar

I will be a dumt person

I will live in a trash bin

and i will fart every hour

i will still love my cat that died and i wil

still love my sister who is a bilionare

My best friend will still be living in a tuna can

And by that time, I will have visited mother country is my trash can

My favorite food will still be rotten tuna

I still won't want to move out of my trashcan

And most importantly, i will be dumb

Joke Decoding #2

Can you solve the secret code and uncover the hidden joke

a	b	c	d	e	f	g	h	i	j	k	l	m
1	2	3	4	5	6	7	8	9	10	11	12	13

n	o	p	q	r	s	t	u	v	w	x	y	z
14	15	16	17	18	19	20	21	22	23	24	25	26

What has a nose and flies but can't smell?

1	14	1	9	18	16	12	1	14	5

Why did the airplane get sent to his room?

2	1	4	1	12	20	9	20	21	4	5

What name do you call a thieving alligator?

1	3	18	15	15	11	15	4	9	12	5

What is brown and sticky?

1	19	20	9	3	11

Opinion Writing

Hamburger

Or

Pizza

Do you like hamburgers or pizza

I like _____

_____

Because _____

_____

_____

_____

_____

_____

_____

_____

_____

_____

_____

Maze #5

Help the koala find the eucalyptus tree!

Flag of Me

Create a unique flag that represents you.
Have fun and be creative!

Do or Does?

Complete these questions using DO or DOES!

1. _____ she play volleyball?

2. _____ we do our homework?

3. _____ he live at that house?

4. _____ you study every day?

5. _____ he brush his teeth?

6. _____ she speak english?

7. _____ it work?

8. _____ they go to school?

9. _____ you play football?

10. _____ you like pizza?

11. _____ they drink water?

12. _____ she play the piano?

13. _____ we listen to music?

14. _____ he read books?

Can you spot the 7 things that are different in these pictures?

Connect The Dots #4

Join the dots to unveil the picture

Spring Word Search

Uncovering the hidden terms in the grid by looking in all directions, including backwards and diagonally

```
Y  J  C  R  B  L  O  S  S  O  M  U
W  O  V  V  T  D  Z  Z  H  K  V  D
L  U  D  C  V  Q  B  T  S  Q  C  C
D  M  Z  Y  E  G  M  W  U  I  G  V
C  J  S  M  G  R  E  E  N  E  R  Y
D  L  U  J  A  X  A  C  S  Y  O  T
K  A  K  W  A  U  I  B  H  L  W  U
R  T  U  L  I  P  S  J  I  I  T  O
I  F  L  O  W  E  R  S  N  R  H  I
L  P  R  J  O  W  Q  I  E  N  D  G
D  B  U  T  T  E  R  F  L  I  E  S
X  A  F  R  E  S  H  N  E  S  S  D
```

Words to Finds

Flowers	Growth	April
Blossom	Warmth	Butterflies
Sunshine	Picnic	Tulips
Greenery	Birds	Freshness

73

Guess the Animal

Can you decipher the identity of the animal based on the clues provided?

1. I am a cunning and clever animal, often associated with trickery in folklore and stories.

2. My fur is typically reddish-brown, but I can come in other colors, too, like silver or black.

3. I have a long, bushy tail that helps me with balance and communication.

4. I'm an omnivore, which means I eat both plants and animals, but I particularly enjoy hunting small mammals and birds.

5. I have excellent night vision, making me a skilled nocturnal hunter

Name

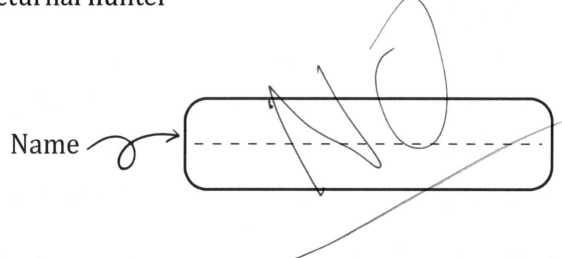

Math Challenge #5

Time to show off your math skills! Help this family find their luggage trailer by coloring only the circles that have even numbers inside!

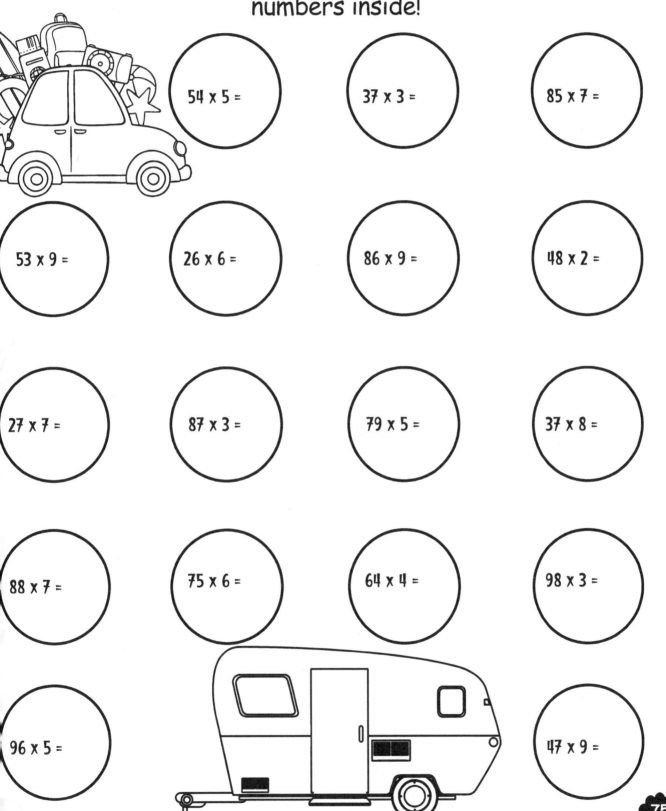

54 x 5 =

37 x 3 =

85 x 7 =

53 x 9 =

26 x 6 =

86 x 9 =

48 x 2 =

27 x 7 =

87 x 3 =

79 x 5 =

37 x 8 =

88 x 7 =

75 x 6 =

64 x 4 =

98 x 3 =

96 x 5 =

47 x 9 =

Circle - Circle - Circle

Unleash your creativity and transform these circles into anything you can imagine!

Joke Decoding #3

Can you solve the secret code and uncover the hidden joke

a	b	c	d	e	f	g	h	i	j	k	l	m
1	2	3	4	5	6	7	8	9	10	11	12	13

n	o	p	q	r	s	t	u	v	w	x	y	z
14	15	16	17	18	19	20	21	22	23	24	25	26

Where do math teachers go on vacation?

20	9	13	5	19		19	17	21	1	18	5

What goes through towns, up hills, and down hills but never moves?

20	8	5		18	15	1	4

What do ghosts eat in the summer?

9		19	3	18	5	1	13

What is a spiders favorite event?

23	5	2	2	9	14	7	19

Hospitals

Across

3. A tube with a nozzle and piston or bulb

5. A small, usually round piece of medicine

7. The act of identifying a disease

8. A friendly machine that shows pictures of your bones and insides.

10. They're like medicine wizards that mix potions and give shots.

Down

1. A qualified practitioner of medicine

2. It's like a magical doctor's wand that listens to your heart.

4. This means you have a high temperature

6. This medicine messenger brings relief in tiny cups.

9. Also known as influenza

Crystal Ball

What do you want to see in your future? Draw or write it in the crystal ball below

Sudoku #5

Easy

```
. . 8 | . . 5 | . . 6
. 9 1 | 3 . . | . . 2
. . 4 | . . . | 8 . .
------+-------+------
. . . | . . . | 9 1 .
8 3 . | 6 . 9 | . . .
. . . | 5 . . | . . 7
------+-------+------
. . 9 | . 6 . | 2 . .
4 . . | . . . | . 7 .
. . . | 3 7 . | 6 . .
```

Easy

```
. . . | 7 . 4 | . . 8
6 . . | . 5 . | . 9 .
. . 3 | 7 . . | . . .
------+-------+------
. . 8 | . 9 . | . . .
. . 9 | . . . | 3 . .
1 . . | . 6 5 | . . .
------+-------+------
. . 6 | 5 . 8 | . . .
3 2 . | . . . | 7 . 5
. . 4 | . . . | . 8 6
```

Medium

```
4 . . | . 7 . | . . .
6 . 4 | . . . | . . 5
8 . 3 | . . . | 4 . 6
------+-------+------
. 7 . | . . . | . . 2
. 2 . | . 6 . | . . .
1 4 9 | . 2 . | . . .
------+-------+------
. . 5 | . . . | 8 9 .
. . 1 | . 6 . | . . 7
. . . | . . . | 5 4 .
```

Medium

```
. . 1 | . . . | . 7 .
5 . . | 2 8 . | . . .
. . 9 | 1 . . | . . .
------+-------+------
. . 9 | 6 . 2 | 3 . .
4 7 . | . . . | . 9 .
. . 2 | . . . | . 5 .
------+-------+------
. . . | 3 . . | . . 4
. 5 . | . . 9 | 6 1 .
. . . | . . . | . . 3
```

81

Anagram Challenge #4

Put your brain to the test and unscramble these christmas terms!!

Atsna Lacsu

- -

Dieenerr

- -

Ridnsoatceo

- -

Sgcskotin

- -

Eilmteost

- -

Drreabggnie

- -

Drawing Activity

Put your artistic talents to use by replicating the image with your own drawing skills

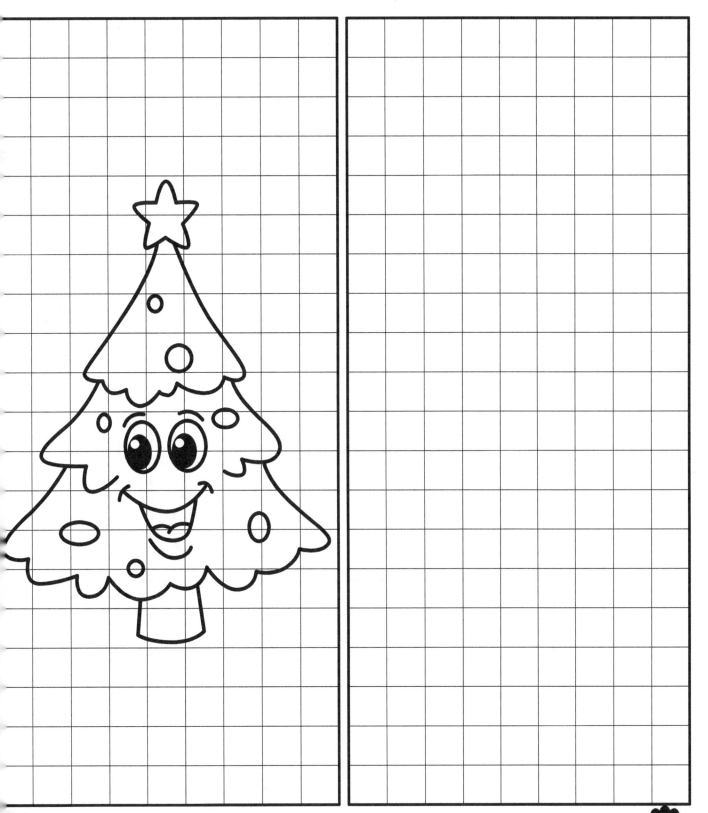

Maze #6

Can you help these to little hedgehogs find their way through the maze to each other?

Can you solve the secret code and uncover the hidden joke

a	b	c	d	e	f	g	h	i	j	k	l	m
1	2	3	4	5	6	7	8	9	10	11	12	13

n	o	p	q	r	s	t	u	v	w	x	y	z
14	15	16	17	18	19	20	21	22	23	24	25	26

What summer vacation destination makes your pet bird sing for joy?

| 20 | 8 | 5 | | 3 | 1 | 14 | 1 | 18 | 25 | | 9 | 19 | 12 | 1 | 14 | 4 | 19 |

What is a cheetahs favorite type of food?

| 6 | 1 | 19 | 20 | | 6 | 15 | 15 | 4 |

What type of cereal do cats eat?

| 13 | 9 | 3 | 5 | | 11 | 18 | 9 | 19 | 16 | 9 | 5 | 19 |

Where do hamburgers go to dance?

| 1 | | 13 | 5 | 1 | 20 | 2 | 1 | 12 | 12 |

Acrostic Poem #3

An acrostic poem is a type of poem where the first letter of each line spells out a word or phrase. All lines should relate to or Describe the poem.
Write an acrostic poem for the word below

Love

L _____

O _____

V _____

E _____

Pizza

Across

1. The hard part around the pizza
6. Deep-dish pizza is from here
7. A cheesy planet with toppings orbiting like stars.
8. Food made from milk that goes on a pizza
10. This spice whisperer adds a sprinkle of enchantment to your slice.

Down

2. The name for one piece of pizza
3. A place that serves pizza
4. Square shaped pizzas
5. It's like a tomato blanket that warms your pizza world.
9. Thick and flat ingredient used to make pizza

Spot The Differences #6

Can you spot the 9 things that are different in these pictures?

Connect The Dots #5

Join the dots to unveil the picture

Weather Word Search

Uncovering the hidden terms in the grid by looking in all directions, including backwards and diagonally

S	U	N	S	H	I	N	E	H	H	F	A
R	T	C	C	K	D	C	U	E	F	B	R
F	U	O	L	M	R	U	T	L	E	E	V
R	D	T	R	O	O	M	L	U	D	K	W
D	D	A	Q	M	U	O	B	N	X	O	U
S	W	C	C	D	G	D	U	C	B	M	N
U	Q	L	H	C	H	H	S	N	A	Y	Z
M	L	I	G	H	T	N	I	N	G	T	M
T	E	M	P	E	R	A	T	U	R	E	L
A	A	A	F	O	R	E	C	A	S	T	E
N	T	T	O	B	L	I	Z	Z	A	R	D
W	S	E	G	H	U	M	I	D	I	T	Y

Words to Finds

Sunshine	Lightning	Climate
Clouds	Temperature	Rainbow
Storm	Humidity	Blizzard
Thunder	Forecast	Drought

Creative Rescue

Quick! Draw something beneath these kids to break their Fall!

My

Solutions

Landforms Word Search

```
P  B  K  P  N  G  R  B  R  W  P  M
V  E  W  V  P  A  Y  S  I  A  M  T
Y  V  R  C  L  R  V  G  S  T  R  P
S  P  G  L  A  C  I  E  R  E  I  F
I  E  T  V  T  N  Z  T  S  R  V  S
B  N  U  O  E  I  Y  E  L  F  E  L
U  I  S  L  A  N  D  O  S  A  R  F
E  N  R  C  U  L  O  I  N  L  Q  N
B  S  L  A  K  E  L  X  Q  L  I  T
K  U  S  N  T  H  N  B  J  L  G  S
W  L  M  O  U  N  T  A  I  N  K  D
V  A  L  L  E  Y  U  G  P  H  X  R
```

Space

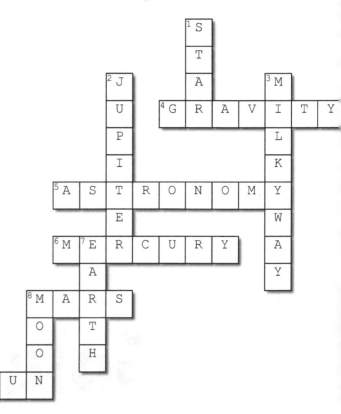

Across:
4. GRAVITY
5. ASTRONOMY
6. MERCURY
8. MARS
9. SUN

Down:
1. STAY
2. JUPITER
3. MILKYWAY
7. EARTH

Maze #1

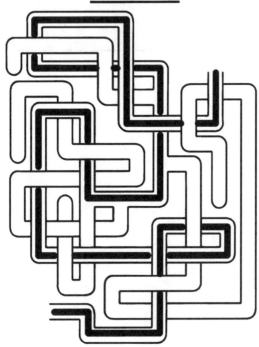

Sudoku #1

Easy

6	1	7	3	4	8	2	9
9	8	6	2	1	7	5	3
7	2	5	8	9	1	4	6
8	5	3	1	7	4	9	2
3	9	8	4	2	6	7	5
2	4	9	6	5	3	1	8
1	6	4	5	3	9	8	7
4	3	2	7	8	5	6	1
5	7	1	9	6	2	3	4

Easy

4	9	5	8	2	7	1	3	6
8	2	6	3	4	1	7	5	9
3	1	7	9	6	5	4	2	8
9	8	2	5	1	6	3	4	7
7	3	4	2	8	9	5	6	1
6	5	1	7	3	4	8	9	2
2	4	8	6	7	3	9	1	5
5	6	3	1	9	8	2	7	4
1	7	9	4	5	2	6	8	3

Medium

4	6	7	1	2	5	3	8	9
9	5	2	4	3	8	7	1	6
1	3	8	6	7	9	2	5	4
5	7	9	3	1	2	4	6	8
3	2	6	9	8	4	5	7	1
8	1	4	5	6	7	9	3	2
7	4	3	8	9	1	6	2	5
2	9	1	7	5	6	8	4	3
6	8	5	2	4	3	1	9	7

Medium

7	3	4	6	2	5	1	9	8
6	9	1	4	3	8	2	7	5
8	5	2	1	9	7	4	6	3
3	6	9	2	8	1	7	5	4
4	7	5	3	6	9	8	1	2
1	2	8	5	7	4	6	3	9
5	8	6	7	4	3	9	2	1
2	4	3	9	1	6	5	8	7
9	1	7	8	5	2	3	4	6

Acrostic Poem #1
(possible answer)

Giggles and laughter, we're all in this together,

As we play and compete, through fair and stormy weather.

Moments of excitement, as we strategize and aim,

Everyone's a winner, in this thrilling, joyful game!

Anagram Challenge #1

United Kingdom

Germany

Australia

South Africa

Argentina

Indonesia

Guess the Country

Ivory Coast

Math Challenge #1

```
 23        47        26
+35       +15       +30
 58        62        56
```

```
 18        59        88
+18       +20       +11
 36        79        99
```

```
 37        55        17
+22       +44       +65
 59        99        82
```

```
 75        12        31
+15       +16       +32
 90        28        63
```

Maze #2

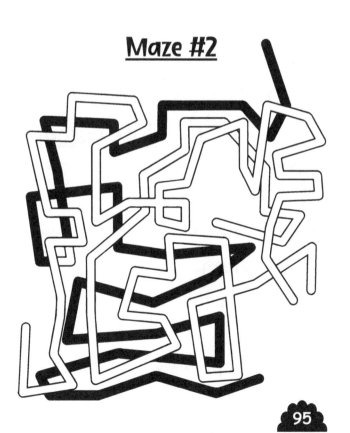

Mythical Creatures

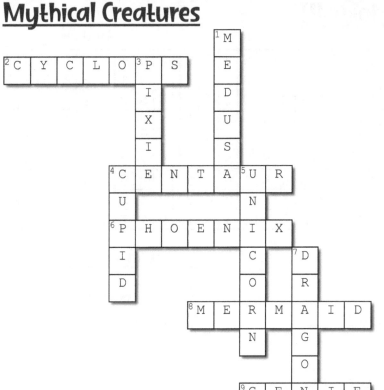

Ocean Life Word Search

Sudoku #2

Easy

3	5	1	8	7	9	2	6	4
7	2	6	4	5	3	8	9	1
9	8	4	6	2	1	5	7	3
1	9	7	2	4	6	3	5	8
6	4	5	3	8	7	9	1	2
2	3	8	1	9	5	6	4	7
4	7	3	9	6	2	1	8	5
5	6	2	7	1	8	4	3	9
8	1	9	5	3	4	7	2	6

Easy

4	3	1	9	8	6	2	7	5
6	7	8	5	3	2	1	4	9
2	9	5	1	4	7	3	6	8
3	5	9	4	2	1	7	8	6
8	2	4	6	7	5	9	1	3
7	1	6	3	9	8	4	5	2
1	4	3	8	5	9	6	2	7
5	6	2	7	1	3	8	9	4
9	8	7	2	6	4	5	3	1

Medium

1	3	8	5	9	2	4	6	7
5	2	4	3	7	6	1	8	9
9	6	7	1	4	8	3	5	2
6	5	1	4	8	9	2	7	3
2	8	9	7	1	3	5	4	6
7	4	3	6	2	5	8	9	1
4	7	6	2	5	1	9	3	8
8	1	5	9	3	7	6	2	4
3	9	2	8	6	4	7	1	5

Medium

4	6	3	8	7	5	1	9	
9	5	2	1	3	6	8	7	
1	7	8	4	9	2	5	3	
7	9	1	6	2	4	3	8	
5	3	4	7	8	1	6	2	
8	2	6	3	5	9	4	1	
6	4	7	2	1	3	9	5	
3	8	5	9	4	7	2	6	
2	1	9	5	6	8	7	4	

Joke Decoding #1

Q. Where do hamsters go on vacation?

A. Hamsterdam

Q. What did the pig say on the beach?

A. I am bacon

Q. What travels around the world but stays in one place?

A. A Stamp

Q. What happens when you wear a watch on a plane?

A. Time flies

Math Challenge #2

 = 3

 = 4

 = 2

 = 1

Anagram Challenge #2

Galaxy
Black Hole
Constellation
Telescope
Solar System
Universe

Guess the Mythical Creature

Phoenix

Dental Health

1. DENTIST (down)
2. FLOSS (down)
3. ROOT (across)
4. TOOTH (down)
5. MOUTHWASH (across)
6. TOOTHFAIRY (across)
7. BACTERIA (down)
8. HYGIENIST (down)
9. SUGAR (down)
10. DENTURES (across)

Maze #3

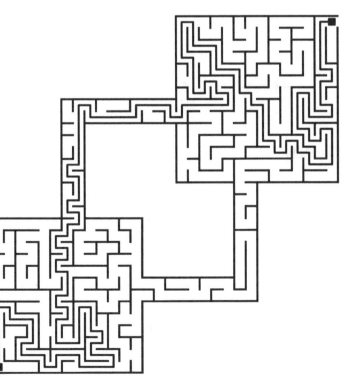

97

Halloween Word Search

```
L A N T E R N  G R A V E
I J F W M G P G R I N Z
M S K B T O I H N O H B
U Z P R D J N O T X S I
S C U O R C O S T U M E
T C M O F M B T T O J G
F O P M L M R Y F E Z G
O B K S O O O L I M R M
C W I T C H H B W L I B
X E N I V A M P I R E Z
D B K C R O W E E Y Y C
M X I K Z D N W V J V U
```

Math Challenge #3

(10) x (1) = 10

(5) x (2) = 10

(6) x (2) = 12

(3) x (4) = 12

(8) x (2) = 16

(4) x (4) = 16

Sudoku #3

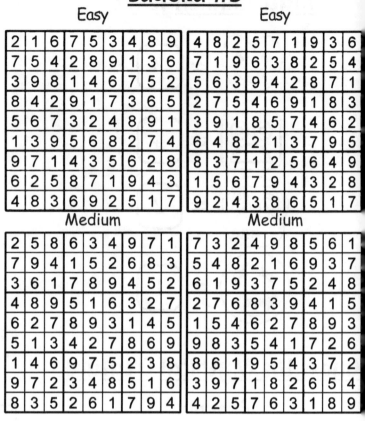

Easy

```
2 1 6 7 5 3 4 8 9
7 5 4 2 8 9 1 3 6
3 9 8 1 4 6 7 5 2
8 4 2 9 1 7 3 6 5
5 6 7 3 2 4 8 9 1
1 3 9 5 6 8 2 7 4
9 7 1 4 3 5 6 2 8
6 2 5 8 7 1 9 4 3
4 8 3 6 9 2 5 1 7
```

Easy

```
4 8 2 5 7 1 9 3 6
7 1 9 6 3 8 2 5 4
5 6 3 9 4 2 8 7 1
2 7 5 4 6 9 1 8 3
3 9 1 8 5 7 4 6 2
6 4 8 2 1 3 7 9 5
8 3 7 1 2 5 6 4 9
1 5 6 7 9 4 3 2 8
9 2 4 3 8 6 5 1 7
```

Medium

```
2 5 8 6 3 4 9 7 1
7 9 4 1 5 2 6 8 3
3 6 1 7 8 9 4 5 2
4 8 9 5 1 6 3 2 7
6 2 7 8 9 3 1 4 5
5 1 3 4 2 7 8 6 9
1 4 6 9 7 5 2 3 8
9 7 2 3 4 8 5 1 6
8 3 5 2 6 1 7 9 4
```

Medium

```
7 3 2 4 9 8 5 6 1
5 4 8 2 1 6 9 3 7
6 1 9 3 7 5 2 4 8
2 7 6 8 3 9 4 1 5
1 5 4 6 2 7 8 9 3
9 8 3 5 4 1 7 2 6
8 6 1 9 5 4 3 7 2
3 9 7 1 8 2 6 5 4
4 2 5 7 6 3 1 8 9
```

Acrostic Poem #2
(possible answer)

Tall and sturdy, reaching for the sky,

Roots deep in the earth, where they firmly li

Embracing all with branches grand.

Each leaf a symbol of life's grace,

Standing strong in every place.

Weather

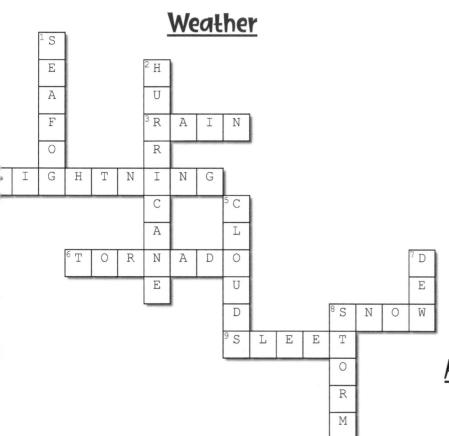

Guess the Landmark

Eiffel Tower

Anagram Challenge #3

Broccoli
Cucumber
Carrot
Turnip
Spinach
Onions

Maze #4

Mythical Creatures Word Search

Math Challenge #4

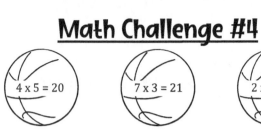

 4 x 5 = 20
 7 x 3 = 21
 2 x 9 = 18

 10 x 5 = 50
 6 x 8 = 48
 7 x 9 = 63

 3 x 7 = 21
 4 x 2 = 8
 1 x 8 = 8

8 x 7 = 56
5 x 6 = 30
3 x 9 = 27

Sudoku #4

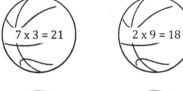

Easy

6	3	7	1	9	5	8	2	4
8	1	4	7	3	2	6	5	9
5	9	2	4	6	8	1	3	7
1	8	5	6	7	9	2	4	3
9	2	3	5	4	1	7	8	6
4	7	6	2	8	3	5	9	1
3	6	1	8	5	4	9	7	2
2	5	9	3	1	7	4	6	8
7	4	8	9	2	6	3	1	5

Easy

1	8	2	4	5	3	7	9	6
4	3	6	2	9	7	5	8	1
7	9	5	1	8	6	2	4	3
3	6	7	9	2	8	1	5	4
8	5	4	6	7	1	3	2	9
2	1	9	3	4	5	6	7	8
6	7	8	5	3	9	4	1	2
9	2	3	7	1	4	8	6	5
5	4	1	8	6	2	9	3	7

Medium

3	2	8	4	5	6	1	7	9
6	1	7	8	9	2	4	5	3
4	5	9	7	1	3	6	8	2
2	9	6	3	8	4	5	1	7
5	7	4	1	2	9	3	6	8
1	8	3	6	7	5	2	9	4
9	4	2	5	6	8	7	3	1
7	3	5	9	4	1	8	2	6
8	6	1	2	3	7	9	4	5

Medium

5	2	1	4	8	6	3	9	7
9	7	6	5	2	3	4	8	1
8	4	3	7	1	9	2	6	5
6	8	7	2	3	5	1	4	9
4	3	9	8	6	1	7	5	2
1	5	2	9	7	4	8	3	6
7	1	4	6	9	8	5	2	3
2	6	5	3	4	7	9	1	8
3	9	8	1	5	2	6	7	4

Family Members

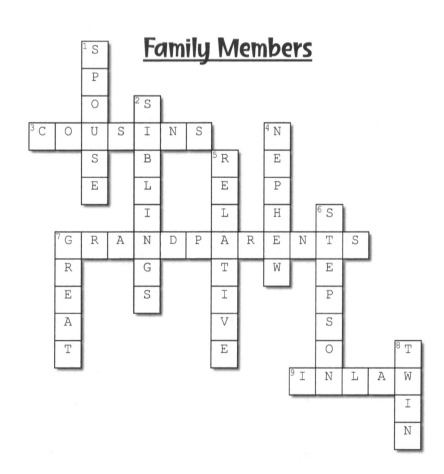

Across/Down answers filled in the crossword grid:
- 1 Down: SPOUSE
- 2 Down: SIBLING
- 3 Across: COUSINS
- 4 Down: NEPHEW
- 5 Down: RELATIVE
- 6 Down: STEPSON
- 7 Across: GRANDPARENTS
- 7 Down: GREAT
- 8 Down: TWIN
- 9 Across: INLAW

Joke Decoding #2

Q. What has a nose and flies but can't smell?

A. An airplane

Q. Why did the airplane get sent to his room?

A. Bad altitude

Q. What name do you call a thieving alligator?

A. A crookodile

Q. What is brown and sticky?

A. A Stick

Maze #5

Guess the Animal

Fox

Spring Word Search

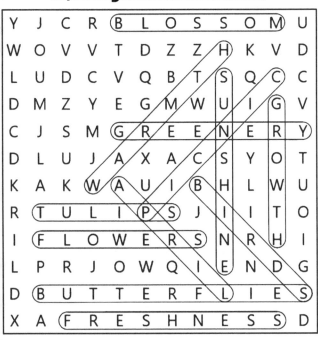

Math Challenge #5

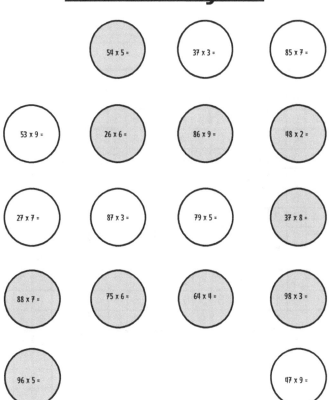

54 x 5 =

37 x 3 =

85 x 7 =

53 x 9 =

26 x 6 =

86 x 9 =

48 x 2 =

27 x 7 =

87 x 3 =

79 x 5 =

37 x 8 =

88 x 7 =

75 x 6 =

64 x 4 =

98 x 3 =

96 x 5 =

47 x 9 =

Joke Decoding #3

Q. Where do math teachers go on vacation?

A. Times Square

Q. What goes through towns, up hills, and down hills but never moves?

A. The road

Q. What do ghosts eat in the summer?

A. I Scream

Q. What is a spiders favorite event?

A. Webbings

Hospitals

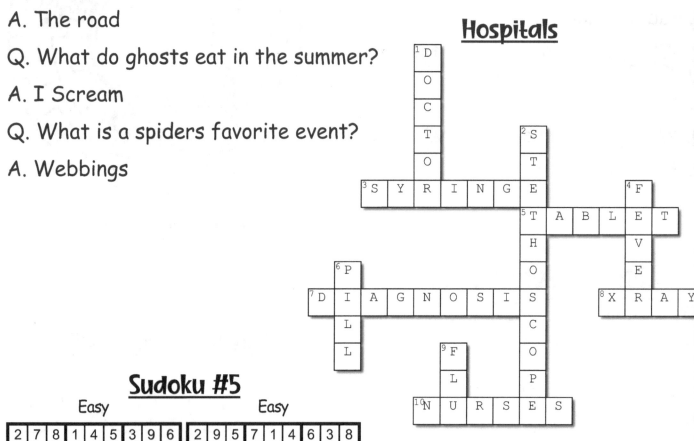

Sudoku #5

Easy

2	7	8	1	4	5	3	9	6
6	9	1	3	7	8	5	4	2
3	5	4	2	9	6	7	8	1
5	4	6	7	2	3	9	1	8
8	3	7	6	1	9	4	2	5
9	1	2	5	8	4	6	3	7
7	8	9	4	6	1	2	5	3
4	6	3	8	5	2	1	7	9
1	2	5	9	3	7	8	6	4

Easy

2	9	5	7	1	4	6	3	8
6	4	1	8	5	3	2	9	7
8	3	7	2	9	6	1	5	4
4	8	3	9	2	7	5	6	1
5	6	9	4	8	1	3	7	2
1	7	2	3	6	5	8	4	9
9	1	6	5	7	8	4	2	3
3	2	8	6	4	9	7	1	5
7	5	4	1	3	2	9	8	6

Medium

4	3	9	6	5	7	8	2	1
6	2	1	4	9	8	3	7	5
8	5	7	3	2	1	9	4	6
3	7	6	1	8	5	4	9	2
9	8	2	7	4	6	5	1	3
5	1	4	9	3	2	7	6	8
1	6	3	5	7	4	2	8	9
2	4	5	8	1	9	6	3	7
7	9	8	2	6	3	1	5	4

Medium

6	2	1	4	9	5	3	7	8
5	3	4	2	8	7	1	6	9
7	8	9	1	3	6	4	2	5
8	9	6	5	2	3	7	4	1
4	7	5	6	1	8	9	3	2
3	1	2	9	7	4	8	5	6
9	6	7	3	5	1	2	8	4
2	5	3	8	4	9	6	1	7
1	4	8	7	6	2	5	9	3

Anagram Challenge #4

Santa Claus

Reindeer

Decorations

Stockings

Mistletoe

Gingerbread

Maze #6

Joke Decoding #4

Q. What summer vacation destination makes your pet bird sing for joy?

A. The Canary Islands

Q. What is a cheetahs favorite type of food?

A. Fast food

Q. What type of cereal do cats eat?

A. Mice Krispies

Q. Where do hamburgers go to dance?

A. A meatball

Acrostic Poem #3
(possible answer)

Laughter and joy, you bring to my days,

Oh, how you light up life's intricate maze.

Vivid and tender, your presence is a gift,

Embracing and warm, my spirits you lift.

Pizza

Weather Word Search

Thank you for purchasing our activity book for kids!

We hope your child had fun completing the activities and that the book brought a little bit of fun and creativity into their day.

If you have a moment, we would really appreciate it if you could leave a review on Amazon. Your feedback helps other parents decide if the book is right for their children, and it helps us improve and reach more families in need of educational and entertaining resources. Plus, it's always nice to hear what people think of our work!

Thank you in advance for your help, and we hope you and your child have a great day!

Kindest regards,

Creative Funland